The Shaping School Culture Fieldbook

The Shaping School Culture Fieldbook

Kent D. Peterson
Terrence E. Deal

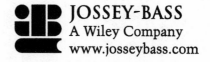

JOSSEY-BASS
A Wiley Company
www.josseybass.com

49285445

2/04

Published by

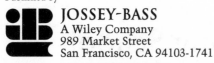 **JOSSEY-BASS**
A Wiley Company
989 Market Street
San Francisco, CA 94103-1741

www.josseybass.com

Jossey-Bass books and products are available through most bookstores. To contact Jossey-Bass directly, call (888) 378-2537, fax to (800) 605-2665, or visit our website at www.josseybass.com.

Substantial discounts on bulk quantities of Jossey-Bass books are available to corporations, professional associations, and other organizations. For details and discount information, contact the special sales department at Jossey-Bass.

We at Jossey-Bass strive to use the most environmentally sensitive paper stocks available to us. Our publications are printed on acid-free recycled stock whenever possible, and our paper always meets or exceeds the minimum GPO and EPA requirements.

Library of Congress Cataloging-in-Publication Data

Peterson, Kent D.
  The shaping school culture fieldbook / Kent D. Peterson,
Terrence E. Deal.—1st ed.
        p. cm.—(The Jossey-Bass education series)
Companion vol. to: Shaping school culture / Terrence E. Deal. 1st
ed. c1999.
Includes bibliographical references (p.   ) and index.
  ISBN 0-7879-5680-5 (pbk. : alk. paper)
  1. Educational leadership—Handbooks, manuals, etc.   2. School
environment—Handbooks, manuals, etc.   3. Educational
change—Handbooks, manuals, etc.   I. Deal, Terrence E.   II. Deal,
Terrence E. Shaping school culture.   III. Title.   IV. Series.
  LB2805.P39   2002
  371.2—dc21   2002003579

FIRST EDITION
PB Printing   10 9 8 7 6 5 4 3 2 1

CONTENTS

ACKNOWLEDGMENTS

A s in our previous work together, we have had a lot of help in putting together this fieldbook. We owe a special debt of gratitude to the teachers and principals whose fine labors have provided most of the examples herein. Practitioners continue to be our best teachers. We hope this book helps repay at least part of the debt.

At Jossey-Bass, Lesley Iura and Christie Hakim continue to serve as the best examples of editorial assistance in a publishing house. Production editor Carolyn Uno helped in many ways to refine and improve the book. As usual, administrative help has been invaluable. Without Homa Aminmadani and Katrina Fox, we would have drowned in the many details needed to pull off a good book. And a special thanks to Erik Peterson, who added illustrations.

We would like to thank the many who have offered support and feedback on our writing and presentations; there are too many to list all of them here. Over the years, Karen Kearney and Laraine Roberts from the California School Leadership Academy and Al Bertani and Ingrid Carney from Chicago have greatly expanded our understanding of professional learning. We appreciate the colleagueship of Pam Robbins, Paul Bredeson, Fran Vandiver, and Joan Vydra, who have been excellent collaborators during our work with groups in workshops and seminars.

Our students have added insights about school culture and leadership. We would especially like to thank Shelby Cosner for her thoughtful reviews of drafts and insights about cultural leaders.

At home, Ann Herrold-Peterson and Sandra Newport Deal provided their usual love and support. Our kids, Erik, Russell, and Scott Peterson and Janie Deal cheered us on when we needed a little boost.

Kent D. Peterson
Terrence E. Deal

THE AUTHORS

Kent D. Peterson is a professor in the Department of Educational Administration at the University of Wisconsin–Madison. He is founding director of the Vanderbilt Principals Institute and the Principals' Leadership Institute at Wisconsin. He consults on the design of leadership development and regularly leads seminars on school leadership and culture in the United States and abroad. In addition to the books he has coauthored with Terrence Deal, he has published over ninety other studies and articles.

Terrence E. Deal is an author, teacher, and consultant. He is the Irving R. Melbo Professor of Education at the Rossier School, University of Southern California, and a consultant to numerous educational, business, military, and religious organizations. He is coauthor of three other books with Kent Peterson, including *The Leadership Paradox: Balancing Logic and Artistry in Schools* (1994) and *Shaping School Culture: The Heart of Leadership* (1999), as well as over twenty other books.

The Shaping School Culture Fieldbook

Introduction and Organization of the Fieldbook

When we gathered cases for our book *Shaping School Culture,* we focused on providing the best examples of a wide variety of school cultures. These examples of what is possible piqued the curiosity of others. Over the past few years, interested leaders have asked us to work with them to learn how to read, assess, and shape their school or district cultures. Drawing on approaches we have used with thousands of principals, as well as new ideas from the leadership literature, we have pulled together concrete ways to approach cultural analysis, assessment, and reinforcement.

This guide is designed to help you reflect on actions, intentions, and understanding in order to hone leadership skills as you shape a better learning environment. It may legitimate some of what you already know and are doing. It also provides activities to develop cultural leadership, and it deepens and concretizes the concept of school culture by connecting it to the success of schools and students.

HOW TO USE THIS BOOK

This guide provides active and reflective approaches for those who wish to improve their school's professional community. Underlying the chapters are three key processes for shaping the cultural ways and traditions.

Leaders must

- Read the culture
- Assess the culture
- Reinforce or transform the culture

Initially, it is critical that leaders read their culture. They need to understand where the culture has come from—the district's or school's history—and understand core features today—the present. During this process, the leader is always interpreting and intuitively determining cultural aspects that are positive, uplifting, and motivating or coming to grips with those that are negative, depressing, and draining.

Second, leaders need to assess the culture by holding up existing ways against other possibilities. They need to identify positive, supportive norms, values, rituals, and traditions. But they should also pinpoint aspects of the culture that may be negative, harmful, or toxic. What positive things need more reinforcement? What negative things need to be changed? As you will learn, you will intuitively begin to assess different aspects as you are reading a culture or engaging in activities to learn more.

Finally, leaders must work to reinforce cultural patterns and ways or transform them. Even the best district or school cultures can wither and die if they are not nurtured and reinforced through daily routines and meaningful rituals. Similarly, moribund or negative aspects of the culture may need to be transformed, changed, or even shed.

THE FIELDBOOK'S ORGANIZERS: DISCUSSIONS, EXAMPLES, ACTIVITIES, AND IDEAS

This book is organized to provide a wide variety of sources of information, inspiration, and suggestions. It can be read and used in a multitude of ways.

Each chapter begins with a discussion of the features of culture and the roles of symbolic leaders. These discussions are often followed by a set of examples to illustrate the ideas.

Next, the book provides specific activities that individuals or a team of teachers or other group can use. Some are specifically designed as group activities, with suggestions for how to organize the session. Others are meant to stimulate reflection; they are often posed as questions for the reader. Almost all the activities can be used with groups; in that case, the questions can become topics for dialogue or group brainstorming.

Interspersed are ideas of interest, which provide the reader with additional issues to consider or to use with staff. Sometimes there are further suggestions for activities, reflections, and plans.

Understanding
School Culture

The Importance of Culture

A great deal of attention is currently being paid to making schools better. Policymakers want to know why we cannot get schools to change more quickly and be more responsive to students' learning needs. The favored response has been to tighten up structures and increase accountability, beef up curriculum standards, test student performance, and provide rewards to schools that measure up and sanctions to those that fall short. In the short term, these solutions may pressure schools to change peripheral practices and raise test scores. In the long term, such external demands will never rival the power of cultural expectations, motivations, and values.

At a deeper level, all organizations, especially schools, improve performance by fostering a shared system of norms, folkways, values, and traditions. These infuse the enterprise with passion, purpose, and a sense of spirit. Without a strong, positive culture, schools flounder and die. The culture of a school or district serves a central role in exemplary performance.

It is the same in any other setting. Whether it is Starbucks coffee or Nordstrom's department store, people function best when they passionately hold to a shared set of key values, central norms, and meaningful traditions.

The key to successful performance is the heart and spirit infused into relationships among people, their efforts to serve all students, and a shared sense of responsibility for learning. Without heart and spirit nourished by cultural ways, schools become learning factories devoid of soul and passion.

Strong, positive school cultures do not just happen. They are built over time by those who work in and attend the school and by the formal and informal leaders who encourage and reinforce values and traditions. Many schools limp along with weak or unfocused cultures due to a paucity of leadership and a lack of concern. But there are just as many other schools that are flourishing because of strong, passionate cultures. These are supported and nourished by teacher leaders and school principals who consciously or unconsciously reinforce the best that the school and its staff can become. The first types of schools are barely surviving; the latter are rich in purpose and abundant in tradition and meaning.

The central concern here is the development of meaningful and productive schools. Leaders must shape and nourish cultures where every teacher can make a difference and every child can learn and where there are passion and a commitment to designing and promoting the absolutely best that is possible.

WHAT IS SCHOOL CULTURE?

The notion of school culture is far from new. In 1932, educational sociologist Willard Waller (1932) argued that every school has a culture of its own, with a set of rituals and folkways and a moral code that shapes behavior and relationships. Parents and students have always detected the special, hard-to-pinpoint esprit of schools.

Students who have attended several schools can pick up the culture immediately as they work to become part of the mix. They know things are different in a positive or negative way—something more than just rules or procedures.

Staff members who walk into a new school also pick it up immediately. They consciously or intuitively begin to interpret unwritten rules, unstated expectations, and underground folkways. Within the first hour of a new assignment, teachers begin to sift through the deep silt of expectations, norms, and rituals to learn what it means to become an accepted member of the school.

The culture is also embedded in an informal cultural network. Staff members often take on roles in that network. Almost every school has its collection of keepers of the values who socialize the newly hired, gossips who transmit information, storytellers who keep the history and lore alive, and heroines or heroes who act as exemplars of core values. In contrast, in toxic cultures one often finds "keepers of the nightmare" who perpetuate everything that has gone awry, rumormongers who share only hostile gossip, negative storytellers who pass on pessimistic history, antiheroines or antiheroes who are harmful exemplars, and others who can destroy positive energy and accomplishments (Deal and Peterson, 1999).

For many educators, the terms *climate* and *ethos* describe this organizational phenomenon. *Climate* emphasizes the feeling and contemporary tone of the school, the feeling of the relationships, and the morale of the place.

We believe the term *culture* best denotes the complex elements of values, traditions, language, and purpose somewhat better and will use it throughout this book. Culture exists in the deeper elements of a school: the unwritten rules and assumptions, the combination of rituals and traditions, the array of symbols and artifacts, the special language and phrasing that staff and students use, the expectations for change and learning that saturate the school's world.

WHERE DOES CULTURE COME FROM?

Beneath the surface of everyday life in schools is an underground river of feelings, folkways, norms, and values that influence how people go about their daily work. This taken-for-granted set of expectations affects how people think, feel, and act. It shapes how they interpret the hundreds of daily interactions of their work lives and provides meaning and purpose in their interactions, activities, and work (Deal and Peterson, 1999).

Where does this aspect of schools come from? Over time, all schools develop a unique personality built up as people solve problems, cope with tragedies, and celebrate successes (Schein, 1985). This personality, or culture, is manifested in people's patterns of behavior, mental maps, and social norms. A simple way of thinking about culture is "the way we do things around here" (Bower, 1966).

WHY IS CULTURE IMPORTANT?

The unwritten tablet of social expectations found in a culture influences almost everything that happens. The culture influences and shapes the ways teachers, students, and administrators think, feel, and act. For example, the following are aspects of the social expectations and values of the staff in a school:

- Whether they think improvement is important
- How motivated they are to work hard

- How they feel when students do not perform well

- How they act in hallways, lounges, and at faculty meetings

- How they dress for different occasions

- What they talk about in public or in private

- The degree of support they give to innovative colleagues

- Whom they go to for ideas or help

- How they feel about their students and colleagues who are different

- Whether they believe all students can learn

- Whether they assume student capacity is determined by background

- The degree to which student learning is dependent on teaching and the curriculum

- Whether they believe collaboration and teamwork is a good thing

- Whether state standards are potentially useful

- Whether they see their daily work as a calling or a job

Every aspect of the school is shaped, formed, and molded by underlying symbolic elements. Although not all cultural aspects are easily shaped by leaders, over time leadership can have a powerful influence on emerging cultural patterns. Being reflective can help reinforce cultural patterns that are positive and transform those that are negative or toxic.

Culture is a powerful web of rituals and traditions, norms, and values that affects every corner of school life. School culture influences what people pay attention to (focus), how they identify with the school (commitment), how hard they work (motivation), and the degree to which they achieve their goals (productivity) (Deal and Peterson, 1999).

A school's culture sharpens the focus of daily behavior and increases attention to what is important and valued. If the underlying norms and values reinforce athletics, the school will focus on that. For example, in one high school, the primary value was a winning football team. The new stadium cost more than five times the budget of the new library. In contrast, in an elementary school in the Midwest, the values were to serve the academic needs of all students. The school thus focused time, energy, and resources on curriculum and instructional strategies that helped all students become readers by the third grade. If the culture supports student learning, that will drive people's attention. Culture sharpens focus.

A school's culture builds commitment and identification with core values. For example, in one school, new teachers were discouraged from identifying with the school by caustic staff members who told stories of poor leadership and hostile parents. The new staff members developed little commitment to the school and came in late to work and left early. In another school, staff felt they were members of a professional community, and even when they were offered higher salaries and new opportunities elsewhere, they refused to leave. If the rituals and traditions, ceremonies and celebrations build a sense of community, the staff, students, and community will identify with the school and feel committed to the purposes and relationships there. Culture builds commitment.

School culture amplifies motivation. When a school recognizes accomplishments, values effort, and supports commitment, staff and students alike will feel more motivated to work hard, innovate, and support change. In one school with an unclear sense of purpose, a lack of an inspiring vision, and few celebrations of accomplishment, staff showed little energy during planning sessions. This was not the case in a Louisiana school where staff members visited one another's classrooms regularly, shared materials and curriculum ideas, celebrated one another's new ideas and accomplishments, and even developed a regional conference on innovative teaching practices. They were motivated not because it was in their job description or contract but because they wanted to. Culture amplifies motivation.

Finally, school culture enhances school effectiveness and productivity. Teachers and students are more likely to succeed in a culture that fosters hard work, commitment to valued ends, an attention to problem solving, and a focus on learning for all students. In schools with negative or despondent cultures, staff have either fragmented purposes or none at all, feel no sense of commitment to the mission of the school, and have little motivation to improve. In many schools with strong professional cultures, the staff share strong norms of collegiality and improvement, value student learning over personal ease, and assume all children can learn if they—teachers and staff—find the curriculum and instructional strategies that work. In these schools, the culture reinforces collaborative problem solving, planning, and data-driven decision making. Positive, professional cultures foster productivity.

WHAT ARE THE KEY FEATURES OF CULTURE?

Culture comprises the deeper, more difficult to identify elements such as norms and values, as well as the more visible features such as rituals and ceremonies. In this book, we will be closely examining the key features of school culture.

> ### Core Elements Addressed in This Book
> - A shared sense of purpose and vision
> - Norms, values, beliefs, and assumptions
> - Rituals, traditions, and ceremonies
> - History and stories
> - Architecture, artifacts, and symbols

We describe the nature of these features, provide group activities for understanding and reading them, illustrate the features with examples from actual schools, and offer reflective questions that individuals or groups of school staff and leaders can ponder.

CAN CULTURE BE SHAPED BY LEADERSHIP?

A key question is, Can culture be shaped by leadership, or is it so amorphous and unalterable that it has a life of its own?

Although school culture is deeply embedded in the hearts and minds of staff, students, and parents, it can be shaped by the work of leaders. As this book demonstrates, one of the key tasks of leaders is shaping culture (Schein, 1985) through myriad daily interactions, careful reflection, and conscious efforts.

The activities in this fieldbook have been used by principals and their faculties to understand the existing cultural patterns and how these can be shaped or altered. Of course, this book is not a panacea. Members of a school must rely on shared values to shape culture in directions that are important, valuable, and meaningful for their school.

Vision and Values

The Bedrock of Culture

M any schools or districts have a set of values that solidly anchor daily activities with a deeper purpose. People know what is important even if it is difficult to articulate what that is. Deeper values and purposes shape a school's vision—its picture of a hoped-for future, its dream of what it can become. These obscure and often veiled dreams provide a deep and rich sense of purpose and direction for an otherwise uncertain future. This mythic side of schools is the "existential anchor" and "spiritual source" for the school's traditions, hopes, and fears (Deal and Peterson, 1999, p. 23).

MISSION AND PURPOSE

At the center of a school's culture are the values that drive long-term planning, resource allocation, and daily work. Many schools have written mission statements to highlight what they are about, but the deeper purposes may be more complex and decidedly more inspirational. Core purposes hidden deep in the cultural fabric provide motivation to teachers, energize leaders to move forward, propel children to learn, and encourage parents and the community to get involved and give their support.

Trying to uncover the authentic mission and purpose may be more difficult than reading a mission statement. Often it requires reading the actions and attitudes of staff and parents, probing plans and daily decisions of students, or uncovering the unstated motivations of teachers and others. In positive cultures, there are strongly held purposes that verge on sacred missions and ennobling ends. In contrast, in toxic cultures, purposes may be base and self-serving. Penetrating the rhetoric to find the more profound elements of a school's mission are key to understanding and shaping the culture.

How might one delve into the school's mission and purpose? Consider the basic concepts.

VALUES

Values are the core of what the school considers important. Values are the standards set for what is "good," what quality means, what defines excellence—what is valued (Ott, 1989). Values shape behavior, decision making, and attention because people attend to what they consider important.

BELIEFS

Beliefs are understandings about the world around us. They are "consciously held, cognitive views about truth and reality" (Ott, 1989, p. 39). In schools, staff, students, and principals hold beliefs about all the major aspects of the organization— beliefs about teacher responsibility for student learning, about student capacity, about ethnicity and social class, about change and innovation, and particularly about the nature of students and their motivation.

NORMS

Norms are the web of expectations that a group holds regarding behavior, dress, language, and other aspects of social life. They are the unstated rules and prescriptions that staff and students are supposed to follow. In some schools, there may be norms about interaction, faculty meeting behavior, how to use preparation periods, and staff development.

ASSUMPTIONS

Assumptions, another key element of the culture, are sometimes viewed as the preconscious "system of beliefs, perceptions, and values" that guide behavior (Ott, 1989, p. 37). Like beliefs, assumptions influence action, thought, and feelings. Assumptions exist relating to the nature of teaching, curriculum, and instruction; different types of children; and leadership.

ACTIVITIES FOR UNCOVERING CULTURAL VALUES, BELIEFS, NORMS, AND ASSUMPTIONS

It is not easy to uncover these often hidden aspects of the culture. But there are several ways leaders can try to identify the core values, beliefs, norms, and assumptions. The following activities can help leaders understand these deeper aspects.

List Six Adjectives to Describe the Culture

Gather the staff, and on sticky notes have each person list six adjectives—one per sticky note—that describe the school culture. Then put the sticky notes on a wall in the school. As a group, start to organize the adjectives into common themes and then into positive adjectives and negative or neutral ones. This activity will give you a conceptual assessment of the culture. Finally, assess the meaning of each grouping. Decide which adjectives should be celebrated and reinforced and which ones should be changed. Use the following space to designate which adjectives should be celebrated and which should be changed.

_____

_____

_____

_____

_____

_____

Assess Mission and Purpose—Walk the Halls and Talk to the Walls

Some of the ways to delve into mission are simpler than others:

Walk the halls. Read mission statements of the past ten years and look for changes over time. List the changes in the mission of your school over the past decade.

_____

_____

_____

_____

_____

_____

Is the mission statement prominently displayed? Is it posted in the office and classrooms and on the letterhead and business cards, coffee cups, T-shirts, and mouse pads? List all the places the mission is displayed at your school.

_____

_____

_____

_____

_____

Do staff, parents, and students know what the mission is? Do they seem excited about it? Describe how each group feels about the mission.

_____

_____

_____

_____

_____

_____

Gather school mottoes, and think about their meaning. Ask all the different stakeholders what they think the school really is trying to accomplish. List the three major purposes mentioned by each group.

_____

_____

_____

_____

_____

Look for what people find joy in. Write down what they get excited about and what stories of success they become emotional about.

_____

_____

_____

_____

_____

Are there rewards for accomplishing the mission and its goals? List them here.

_____

_____

_____

_____

_____

_____

_____

Walk the hallways when everyone is gone, and reflect on what the walls say about what is really important. Jot them down here.

_____

_____

_____

_____

_____

_____

_____

Diagram the School's Purpose and Mission

Are there consistent patterns in the views of what is a valued mission in the school? Are there broad differences? Are there deep purposes (such as authentic learning) or narrow goals (for example, improving reading scores)? On the facing page, draw a diagram or picture of the purposes you uncovered:

Come Up with a Song for Your Culture

Identify a song that represents the school or district's essence or a major feature of the culture. Some of the songs (or their identifying lyrics) mentioned by educators include these:

"Anticipation"

"Respect"

"(I Can't Get No) Satisfaction"

"Eight Days a Week"

"9 to 5"

"Hard Day's Night"

"Wind Beneath My Wings"

"We Are Family"

"The Hero Is in You"

"The World Is a Rainbow"

"The Way We Were"

"On the Road Again"

"We Are the Champions"

"Let's Get Ready to Rumble"

"The Power of the Dream"

"Bad to the Bone"

"Imagine"

"The Long and Winding Road"

"I Will Survive"

"Movin' on up a Little Higher"

"Lean on Me"

"Ball of Confusion"

"We Are the World"

"You Can't Always Get What You Want"

"Don't Fence Me In"

"Yesterday"

"Sixteen Tons"

"Whistle While You Work"

"Ain't No Stoppin' Us Now"

"Living La Vida Loca"

"If I Could Fly"

"Take This Job and Shove It"

"It's a Small World"

"Help!"

"My Way"

"Tomorrow"

"It Don't Come Easy"

List songs representing positive aspects of culture:

_____

_____

_____

_____

_____

_____

List songs representing negative aspects of culture:

_____

_____

_____

_____

_____

Idea: During major reform projects, stress and conflict often arise. Use this technique of identifying songs to assess how the culture is coping with major changes.

Idea: If the staff comes up with mostly negative songs, ask them what song they would like to represent the culture if they could reinvigorate the school.

Write an Advertisement for Your School

Divide the staff randomly into groups of four or five, and have each group write an advertisement for the school. Ask them to imagine that they are responsible for developing an ad to be published in the local newspaper or its Sunday magazine. In a relatively few number of words, they must try to capture the school's spirit, purposes, and accomplishments. They should include pictures, symbols, photos, or quotations, or a combination of these, that convey meaning and would attract new students, teachers, or parents. Use this space for your advertisement.

Put the advertisements on chart paper, and post them on the walls. Have each group pick a spokesperson to present its ad.

As you listen to the ads, think about which major themes are repeated and what values are reinforced.

Idea: As a next step, put these themes into a digital video advertisement with a maximum length of sixty seconds. Use whatever symbols or local actors—students, teachers, volunteers, or others in the school community—that people feel best represent the school. Show the ad on local access television or put on the school's or district's home page.

Design a Symbolic Representation—A Heraldry Shield

In ancient times, kings and queens would have court artists design a heraldry shield that included symbols of values, accomplishments, and their honor or might.

As individuals or in small groups, design a heraldry shield depicting your school's core values and purposes. Discuss the symbols and meaning in what people have created. Draw the shield here:

Encourage Metaphorical Thinking

It is useful to encourage creative approaches to understanding deeper interpretations and understandings. Metaphorical thinking provides an engaging way to read the culture. Here's an approach that has worked with school leaders around the country.

Gather the staff, students, or parents together, and ask everyone to write a metaphor for the school (adapted from Gordon, 1961). Distribute sticky notes (three by five inches or larger) to everyone, and ask them to complete this metaphor:

If my school were an animal, it would be a _____, because

_____

_____

_____

_____

Emphasize the importance for giving reasons for the choice. Staff members sometimes select the same animal, but for different reasons. For example, one staff member for a school said the school was like an octopus "because it had arms reaching in every direction and no backbone." Another staff member also picked an octopus, but "because it has strong arms reaching out for nutrients and connected in the center."

Stick the metaphors on a wall (or print them up if there is some conflict among the staff, so that everyone remains anonymous) and look for underlying meanings or themes in the metaphors. For example, in one school, many of the metaphors were about female predators (lionesses, bears, cheetahs). Many had a common theme of care and nurturing for the young but hostility toward other adults who might come close. The discussion turned toward how staff members could become more respectful and supportive of each other.

In another school, a number of the metaphors identified animals that changed during the life cycle (chameleons, butterflies, tadpoles). The staff felt proud of its ability to cope with changes in their school.

Draw a Picture of Your Culture

A good initial exercise to help read the culture is to draw a picture representing the school. Have each person draw a representative depiction of the culture using pictures, words, symbols, and color. A simple sheet of paper eight and a half by eleven inches will do. Encourage creativity and respect for those whose art skills are limited. Draw your picture here:

Have groups share their pictures and what they mean. Look for implicit themes such as collaboration, support, nurturant relationships, and negative or hostile elements. Discuss as a group what the overall view of the school is based on the pictures.

Identify the Heroines and Heroes of Your School

Every school has a set of exemplars—heroines and heroes. These members of the cultural network represent role models for the culture.

Use the following space to identify the heroines and heroes of your culture. Learn what they have accomplished, and find time to recognize and celebrate what they represent to the school.

School heroines and heroes:

_____

_____

_____

_____

_____

_____

Their accomplishments:

_____

_____

_____

_____

_____

_____

Ways to recognize and celebrate their exemplary work:

_____

_____

_____

_____

_____

_____

_____

Ritual and Ceremony

Culture in Action

A life devoid of ritual and ceremony would be one without richness and zest. The small daily rituals of our lives provide time for reflection, connection, and meaningful experience. Imagine a day without morning coffee or a glance at the newspaper, without the late afternoon break with colleagues, absent the nightly walk with a loved one. Rituals help keep us connected, foster renewal, and provide opportunities to bond with others we work or live with.

Rituals and ceremonies often occur in regular patterns over the year, punctuating and providing bookends for the flow of months. Much richness and connection would be lost if we had no opening school ceremony, Halloween, Thanksgiving, Christmas, Cinco de Mayo, Kwanzaa, Hanukkah, Easter, Passover, New Year's Eve, or Homecoming.

Without ceremonies and traditions to mark the passage of time, honor the accomplishment of valued goals, and celebrate the possibilities of new hopes and dreams, our lives would stagnate, dry up, and become empty of meaning and purpose. These episodic cultural events help keep us all connected to the deeper values of our labor and the institution where we have committed our lives. Without ceremonies, traditions, and rituals, we can easily lose our way in the complexity of everyday life at work.

Rituals and ceremonies help make the intangible graspable and the complex understandable. They allow us to act out meaning and values that would otherwise be difficult to understand and feel. Communal events help bond us together.

Social events are the outward expression of the deeper possibilities of culture and its core values. They are to school culture what the movie is to the script, what the concert is to the score, and what the sculpture is to the values of the artist (Deal and Kennedy, 1982).

Education, that is, seeing that children learn in a safe and supportive environment, remains one of the most complex and challenging of all social endeavors. In many ways, building cars, designing ships, and developing software are simple in comparison. Ritual and ceremony are probably more important in schools than in businesses because the product and the services are so complex and the important outcomes hard to measure. Because of this, leaders must bring ritual and ceremony into the lives of teachers and students. These symbolic social events help staff members through the daily routines and demands of teaching and foster professional community and a common spirit of caring and camaraderie.

In this period of intense scrutiny and state accountability, schools need to rejuvenate rituals and energize key traditions to keep spirit and soul alive. Learning for both students and teachers is enhanced through meaningful traditions, frequent ritual, and community ceremonies that nurture and nourish cohesion, motivation, and focus.

RITUALS

Rituals are processes or daily routines that are infused with deeper meaning. They are more than just technical actions. Rituals help transform common experience into uncommon events. Every school has hundreds of routines, from the taking of attendance in the morning to the exiting procedures of the afternoon. When these routine events can be connected to a school's deeper mission and values, they summon spirit and reinforce cultural ties; for example,

- Some schools provide welcome kits for students filled with school supplies, books, and a videotape about the school. Other schools give each student a buddy or mentor.

- At Ganado Primary School in Ganado, Arizona, visitors are taken on a tour by an articulate Navajo tour guide who shows them through the hallways and into the central IMC with its display of superb Navajo rugs from local weavers.

- In a school in the Midwest, new teachers have a mentor who tells them the history of the school, takes them on a tour of the community, and shows them the informal rules.

- In another school, new staff members are given a school coffee cup and provided a list of all the accomplishments and awards the school and its teachers have received as a way of connecting them to the culture.

TRADITIONS

Traditions are significant singular events that have a special history and meaning and occur year in and year out. Unlike ceremonies, they need not be large communal events. Traditions are part of the history of the school and tie people to its cultural roots. There are many traditions in schools. Here are some examples:

- Meeting in the summer for a barbecue and games
- Holding regular faculty retreats to plan school improvement efforts
- Arranging school overnights or camping trips for students
- Painting a rock by seniors
- Holding a school art auction for parents and community
- Having special foods or speeches during ceremonies
- Having the school storyteller at retirement parties
- Framing staff and student accomplishments and art
- Celebrating a school's benefactor in a ceremony
- Wearing academic robes at graduation
- Making food for a fellow staff member when there has been illness or tragedy in that person's family

When people have traditions that they value and appreciate and that occur with regularity through the year, they have a foundation for weathering challenges, difficulties, and change. Following are some more examples of traditions:

- In one Wisconsin school, every adult who works in the school goes to the kitchen and shares cinnamon toast in the morning.
- In another school, teachers traditionally share workshop reports, evaluations, and stories after returning from professional development opportunities.
- In one school, the staff starts the faculty meeting by telling stories—sometimes funny, sometimes serious—about students in their classes.
- At Coral Springs Middle School in Florida, when Fran Vandiver was principal, faculty meetings would start with a story. Vandiver would tell a story of a teacher or staff member who had done something special to help a student or parent and then present that person with a school coffee cup.

CEREMONIES

Most schools have formal ceremonies that mark transitions in the school year. These periodic communal events bind people to each other and shape unwritten cultural values.

Ceremonies are complex, culturally sanctioned events that provide a welcome spiritual boost. Through ceremonies, the school uses communal events to celebrate successes, communicate its values, and recognize special contributions of staff, parents, and students. Each season of the year can provide time to communicate ceremonially the deeper symbolic glue that binds a school together.

ACTIVITIES TO READ, ASSESS, AND REINFORCE OR TRANSFORM RITUALS, TRADITIONS, AND CEREMONIES

Assess School Rituals

Schools have many types of rituals. You can understand and shape the culture by reflecting on common rituals. Ask yourself what your rituals are and what they communicate. This section considers several different types of rituals. Determine which of these are in your school, and reflect on their meaning.

Greeting Rituals

Every organization specifies ways to greet people and bid them goodbye. These rituals communicate how a school values various groups. What is particularly important is how parents or new staff members are welcomed.

How are new teachers acknowledged in faculty meetings? How are they introduced?

_____

_____

_____

_____

_____

_____

How are new students and their parents or caregivers greeted? What are they told about the school? What are they given to help them connect and adjust?

_____

_____

_____

_____

_____

_____

Transition Rituals

Transition rituals provide staff members with a way to move from one role, program, or approach to another or to end an era symbolically. Without transition rituals, the sense of loss can increase and cause problems.

Does your school have significant rituals for the major transitions during the year: as school begins, after winter break, at the end of the year? What are they like? If you do not have them, suggest some.

_____

_____

_____

_____

_____

_____

What are the rituals when staff members receive tenure, work for five or ten years at the school, or retire?

_____

_____

_____

_____

_____

Testing Preparation Rituals

Most schools are facing increased testing and accountability. Schools have always held pep rallies before athletic contests, and now many are holding rallies before testing periods. School rituals recognizing challenges ahead can motivate effort and ease tensions.

What special rituals take place before testing periods—for example, a school pep rally? A special edition of the newsletter? Pins to encourage effort?

_____

_____

_____

_____

_____

Initiation Rituals

All cultures have rituals for newcomers. Whether one is aware of it or not, we initiate new people into the school through words and deeds. How people are initiated influences their understanding of the school's values and their commitment to the organization.

Are new staff members initiated into the school through formal mentoring or informal induction? What are some of the ways in which this is done?

_____

_____

_____

_____

_____

_____

What information is provided about the norms and values of the school and its vision and dreams?

_____

_____

_____

_____

_____

_____

Are there formal initiation rites to connect new staff members to the existing culture? Write down some of them here.

_____

_____

_____

_____

_____

_____

Closing and Ending Rituals

The closing of a school and the ending of a program are key times to hold rituals. These are always difficult times and need to be recognized symbolically and socially. Without rituals, the needed psychological closure may not occur.

Recall the last time a program ended, a staff member left, a textbook "retired," or a unit closed. How was it affirmed?

_____

_____

_____

_____

_____

What rituals most helped people through those endings?

_____

_____

_____

_____

_____

Are there endings that have not had proper closure? A ritual may be needed to promote healing and letting go. What could you design to gain some closure?

_____

_____

_____

_____

_____

_____

Identify and Interpret Your Traditions

Traditions are events or actions that occur from year to year that build a sense of continuity, reinforce values, and build community. School leaders actively assess their traditions and make them more meaningful.

What are your school's traditions, and what meaning do they have for faculty, students, and community?

_____

_____

_____

_____

_____

_____

Identify Core Traditions and Ceremonies

Following are some ceremonies found in schools. Track the ceremonies in your school over the year. Identify which of these traditions and ceremonies occur in your school and what they celebrate.

Opening day ceremonies to rebind staff and build community:

_____

_____

_____

_____

_____

Seasonal ceremonies during natural cycles (such as Cinco de Mayo, Black History Month, or Homecoming):

_____

_____

_____

_____

_____

Management ceremonies to accomplish administrative tasks (presentation of the yearly school goals):

_____

_____

_____

_____

_____

_____

Integrative ceremonies to meld social, religious, and ethnic groups:

_____

_____

_____

_____

_____

Recognition ceremonies to pay tribute to the special accomplishments of individuals and groups, thereby forging pride and respect:

_____

_____

_____

_____

_____

Homecoming ceremonies to reconnect graduates with the school and to develop a sense of history and continuity:

_____

_____

_____

_____

_____

Special ceremonies to mark the beginning or end of unique events:

_____

_____

_____

_____

_____

_____

Memorial ceremonies to remember the contributions of staff, students, or community members who are no longer with the school:

_____

_____

_____

_____

_____

_____

What are all the ceremonies at your school? What message, value, or norm do the ceremonies communicate and reinforce?

_____

_____

_____

_____

_____

_____

Map Traditions and Ceremonies over the Year

Ceremonies are key features of the culture occurring at different times in the year. Knowing when ceremonies are scheduled can provide a picture of their distribution throughout the school year.

Write down the large and small traditions and ceremonies over the year in the space that follows, and then construct a timeline. Note any periods of time that have few of these important events. Be especially aware of any ceremonies or traditions that are either weak or dead. It may be time to drop or resuscitate them.

August _____

_____

_____

September _____

_____

_____

October _____

_____

_____

November _____

_____

_____

December _____

_____

_____

January _____

_____

_____

February _____

_____

_____

March _____

_____

_____

April _____

_____

_____

May _____

_____

_____

June _____

_____

_____

July _____

_____

_____

Redesign Successful School Ceremonies

Ceremonies offer the opportunity to showcase successes, reinforce effort, and cement the social relationships that are so important to making schools caring, safe, and productive. Ceremonies can celebrate the start of the school year, recognize the accomplishments of students and staff, provide closure to long careers at retirements, and at other times. Following are the types of elements one finds in various ceremonies (Deal and Peterson, 1999):

- A special and value-linked purpose

- Symbolic clothing and adornments

- Symbols, signs, banners, or flags

- Stories of history, accomplishment, and unusual effort

- A distinctive manner of speaking or presentation

- An invocation of deeper purpose and values

- Attention to who is invited and where they sit

- Recognition of those who have shown exemplary commitment

- Appropriately chosen and varied music

- A carefully selected, attractive setting

- Delicious food or drink

- Value-filled language and commentary

- Meaningful symbols and artifacts

- Ritual acts and ongoing traditions

- The recounting of myths, legends, or stories about the school

Ceremonies should mirror and signal the values of the school and the vision for the future. Following are questions to ask as you design or redesign a ceremony. Space is provided for you to jot ideas or notes as you think about each question.

What message is being sent?

_____

_____

_____

How is the school bonding with the community?

_____

_____

_____

Who is involved?

_____

_____

_____

Are the school's core values communicated in multiple ways?

_____

_____

_____

Are there opportunities for the group to recommit to the mission?

_____

_____

_____

Are stories told of accomplishment and dedication?

_____

_____

_____

Are new members appropriately recognized?

_____

_____

_____

Is the costume or dress appropriate and symbolic?

_____

_____

_____

Are symbols present that communicate values and expectations?

_____

_____

_____

Are school artifacts included?

_____

_____

_____

Are the location and setting appropriately serious or fun?

_____

_____

_____

Is there music to reinforce the tone and feeling of the event?

_____

_____

_____

Is carefully selected food or drink part of the ceremony?

_____

_____

_____

Are elders recognized and celebrated?

_____

_____

_____

Does the sequence of events provide the right flow of ideas, actions, movement, and values?

_____

_____

_____

Is the tone of speeches, music, and stories appropriate to the symbolic meaning of the event?

_____

_____

_____

Identify the Elements and Meaning of Ceremonies

It is key to assess the meaning and purpose of all aspects of the ceremony.

In the space below, list on the left the elements of one of your key ceremonies. Next, reflect on the symbolism and meaning of that element, and detail it on the right. Finally, identify any elements that do not communicate what you would like them to and suggest ways to improve their message.

Ceremonial Element	Symbolism, Meaning, or Value

Reflect on Dead or Dying Ceremonies

Not all ceremonies maintain their vibrancy and purpose. Some are dead (and ought to be ended), but others that are dying should be revived and resuscitated.

Are there any ceremonies in your school that no longer have meaning, are simply seen as requirements, or reinforce negativity? Some ceremonies are dead, dying, or dormant. Decide what to do to revive those moribund ceremonies.

A dead ceremony that you want to revive:

_____

_____

_____

_____

_____

_____

_____

_____

A dead ceremony that needs to be buried:

_____

_____

_____

_____

_____

_____

_____

_____

History and Stories

The Importance of the Past

HISTORY

It is sometimes easy for us to understand the influence of the past when we look at generations: the Depression and World War II deeply shaped the generation of the early 1920s. The war in Vietnam and the civil rights movement molded the baby boom generation. The September 11 attacks are key events for those living now. But past events also deeply shape the culture of organizations.

School culture is built up over time as people work together, play together, fight together, cry together, and laugh together. The most profound values and relationships come into being as staff members face crises, deal with tragedy, make mistakes, enjoy success, and recognize accomplishments—problems solved and conflicts resolved. The end of a leadership team, the death of a student or the life-threatening illness of a staff member, the implementation of a new combined math-science curriculum, or the selection as a National School of Excellence—all of these events can affect indelibly core norms and values.

The past is truly never far away. People remember (and are reminded in the stories that are told) the past and the feelings it produces. The songwriter Jim Steinman uses the metaphor of the automobile rearview mirror to recognize the closeness of meaningful past events and relationships. He notes in one of his songs, "Objects in the mirror are closer than they appear."

It is critically important for leaders to know and understand the history of the school. Just as doctors and psychotherapists need to understand the history of a patient, leaders need to know events that have shaped the psyche of the school.

Why is this so important? Core features of a culture are molded over time through critical incidents, emotional events, and profound accomplishments. Over time, values and folkways are crystallized and buttressed through use and reinforcement. Beliefs about what works and what does not are molded by experience and then hardened by time. Stories carry the genetic code, informing new staff members about "how we do things around here," reinforcing certain forms of behavior, and crystallizing beliefs about collegiality, hard work, and change.

Over time, past events take on mythic proportions, and legend becomes reality. Sometimes the past is viewed as positive, hopeful, and energizing; at other times, the past is seen as negative, pessimistic, and discouraging. Every school has successes and missteps or failures. How it deals with the past shapes its present and future.

Cultural Assessment

Cultural patterns and traditions evolve over time. What forces nudge a culture in one direction or another? Formal and informal leaders articulate direction and purpose through words and deeds. Crises and controversies forge new values and norms in the ongoing crucible of tension and strife. People, through everyday activities, spin unstated rules governing relationship and conflict. Planned change leaves its own legacy of traces and mementos. Cycles of birth, death, and renewal leave a rich sediment of secrets and sentiment.

How Schools Deal with History

Like individuals, schools have varied responses to the past. Some celebrate history in public festivals. Others have negative histories, and staff members continue to harbor anger about past events. Wounds are left to fester, infecting the present with a pessimistic, negative tone. This spawns widespread fear that problems of the past will repeat themselves in hurtful ways.

Still other schools suffer from historical amnesia. People refuse to acknowledge and honor the past, believing that only the present and future are important. They are in organizational denial.

A learning organization is one that mines past and present experiences for important lessons and principles. Through trial and error, people learn what works and what does not. Across time, triumphs and tragedy accumulate in cultural codes—a legacy of shared wisdom that lets people know what is the best or right thing to do. Recounting history transmits these important precepts, giving meaning to cultural practices and ways.

Without roots, an organization wanders aimlessly, often repeating past mistakes and failing to learn from success. As an example, a Broward County, Florida, principal was describing a past year's disaster. She was trying to instill in teachers a sense of empowerment that they could take charge and make decisions on their own, and so she arranged for a consultant from a local bank to offer a day-long session on empowerment. But in the midst of the session, teachers revolted and asked the consultant to leave. They did not see his message as relevant or of much help. The principal was devastated and vowed never again to try to empower the school's teachers. As her story ended, an observer said, "Wait a minute. Didn't that event demonstrate that teachers could take charge? In trashing the empowerment session, teachers empowered themselves. What a great lesson—as long as it is made explicit. You thought you failed. In fact, you were a resounding success. Why not write the history that way?"

How does the history of the school affect its culture today? As we noted in the definition, the elements and character of organizational culture are initiated at inception, shaped by critical incidents, forged by controversy and conflict, and crystallized by use and reinforcement (Schein, 1985; Deal and Kennedy, 1982). The culture becomes what it is over time as people cope with problems, establish routines and rituals, and develop traditions and ceremonies that strengthen and sustain the underlying norms, values, and beliefs. Over time, the informal crystallizes into shared norms and values. Core assumptions become taken-for-granted rules that cannot be broken.

ACTIVITIES TO ASSESS THE HISTORY OF YOUR SCHOOL
Get an Initial Reading of the School
A school leader can get an initial reading of a school by asking a few key questions, such as the following, about its founding, traditions, and past key events of the school.

How long has the school existed?

_____

_____

Why was it built, and who were the first inhabitants?

_____

_____

_____

_____

What was the school's design and architecture supposed to convey?

_____

_____

_____

_____

Who has had a major influence on the school's direction? What were that person's core values?

_____

_____

_____

_____

_____

What critical incidents occurred in the past, and how were they resolved, if at all?

_____

_____

_____

_____

_____

_____

What were the previous principals, teachers, and students like in the 1970s? In the 1980s? In the 1990s?

_____

_____

_____

_____

_____

_____

Investigate Additional Elements of School History

Additional elements of history should also be investigated to understand the culture. Questions on the following topics offer further guides to the examination of a school's history.

Leadership. Formal and informal leaders help provide direction through a sense of purpose and mission. Who were the formal and informal leaders of the school? What did they stand for? What new approaches, structures, or ideas did they bring to the school? If the school is relatively new, who were the founding principal and teacher leaders?

_____

_____

_____

_____

_____

_____

_____

Crises and controversies. Crises, controversies, or conflicts forge norms and values of the culture by hardening assumptions in the crucible of strife. What were the major crises, controversies, or conflicts that staff members had to face over time? What was the source of the difficulty? How did staff members resolve the conflicts? Did they hold the anger for years or address the differences directly and honestly? Did part of the staff leave because of the disagreements? Was some accommodation or compromise reached to rebuild a sense of community? Are the issues still part of an ongoing set of concerns and negative memories?

_____

_____

_____

_____

_____

_____

_____

_____

People, personalities, and relationships. Personalities of people inhabiting an epoch in the school's history establish ways of interacting with others. They form unstated rules for relationships and interaction. Who were the people who made the school what it is? What were they like? How did they treat others in the building? What kinds of relationships developed over time and became the ways of treating people, staff, students, and parents?

_____

_____

_____

_____

_____

_____

_____

_____

Birth, death, and renewal. All schools face waves of birth, death, and renewal among people, values, and programs. How these critical borders are traversed affects future transitions. How were new programs or instructional philosophies initiated, implemented, and, at times, ended? How was the sadness of losing a staff member (through transfer, death, or retirement) dealt with? What were the incidents of renewal as the school took on exciting and successful new programs, people, or plans?

_____

_____

_____

_____

_____

_____

_____

_____

_____

_____

Changes, modifications, and adjustments. Change is never easy. The aftermath of positive and negative memories lingers, sometimes for decades. The ways the school dealt with changes in programs or people, modifications of goals or educational philosophies, and adjustments of schedules and methodologies are often remembered and can surface whenever new changes are introduced. What are the changes that invoke strong memories for staff, students, and community? What have been changes in curriculum, instruction, or the use of time and materials? How have new technologies been introduced and used? How have changes in the types of students in the school been greeted? How have shifts in the goals, outcomes, or standards been embraced by staff, students, and community?

_____

_____

_____

_____

_____

_____

_____

_____

_____

_____

How schools face their history. Like people, schools have varied responses to critical incidents that make up shared history. Often, staff reactions to the past parallel reactions to death and dying (Kübler-Ross, 1969). Some staff members feel angry that the past events occurred. Others are in denial, refusing to acknowledge that anything happened. Some experience fear; they worry that past problems may materialize again. Who might be stuck in an early stage of the grieving process?

_____

_____

_____

_____

_____

_____

_____

_____

How schools learn for the future. Some educators use history to learn for the future. Those who have dealt with history directly often feel internalized acceptance, power, and control. They know that they have learned from experience and can cope with many things life throws at them. They have transformed negative experiences into personal centeredness. Successful schools nourish the heritage that brought them to the present. In doing so they reconfirm Clark's (1972) observations of the reason unique colleges succeed. These organizations relied on a saga or historical narrative to unite faculty, students, administrators, staff, and alumni into a beloved institution. That is also possible in elementary and secondary schools. Does your school have any special myths or sagas of its history?

_____

_____

_____

_____

_____

_____

_____

_____

_____

Create a Visual History

One of the most important aspects of a school is its history. Often new staff members do not know about the important people, events, and issues that have shaped the school over time. A useful technique is to have the staff develop their shared history and display it on chart paper.

One approach is to involve the entire staff in creating the historical visual display. To begin, divide the staff into small groups by the decades in which they joined the school (not when they first became educators if it was at another school). In many schools, a large proportion were hired in the 1990s, so divide this group into the early 1990s (1990–1995) and after 1995 (1996-today). Give each group some chart paper and a marker, and have them brainstorm what happened in those years. Their description points could include these:

- Major events in the school and district
- Key formal and informal leaders
- Ideas about curriculum, instruction, and assessment
- Characteristics of students and community
- Key successes, challenges, or crises
- Architectural or social changes in the school
- New rituals, traditions, or ceremonies
- The quality of social relationships in the school
- People, personalities, and social interaction
- Special events that shaped staff or student concerns
- Clothing, hairstyles, and music of the decade

Post the completed historical charts chronologically, and have a spokesperson from the group tell the story of each decade. Have them add detail to make the decade come alive. Go through all the decades, and think about the school's history. Look for clues about the values that have transcended time and help define the culture as it is today. In some schools, this is a cathartic experience. In others, it provides new staff members with a deeper understanding of senior staff members.

Keep the history. One school printed up its history and made it available to new staff members. Another school captured stories and edited them into a video of the school's history for use at fall homecoming and other events.

Every important organization has a history—that set of events, people, values, and crises that made it what it is. School leaders should make sure that there is a record of what happened to give the school a sense of its roots.

STORYTELLING

Stories are powerful ways to communicate important information about a school. Too often, professionals believe that quantitative, concrete descriptions of the school—number of teachers, size of the school, grade levels served—are the best way to characterize the enterprise. Concrete data are extremely useful for planning and decision making, but stories rich in metaphor and meaning are perhaps a more powerful way to tell people about the school.

Stories are key cultural elements, and they serve many purposes. They can help initiate new staff members into cultural understanding, provide laughter or tears needed to get through a difficult situation, and reinforce core values and purposes. Stories are powerful in part because people can easily remember and be moved by stories that are vivid, meaningful, and clear.

Every school has staff members who tell stories, and some have identified storytellers as part of their cultural network. Providing time for storytellers can reinforce history and support mission.

Hank Cotton, a principal of Cherry Creek High School in Cherry Creek, Colorado, was a superb storyteller who communicated his values in stories. Each story had a theme—for example,

- The importance of innovation
- The need for hard, continual work to achieve success

- The ways that quiet students or teachers can achieve success through continual struggle
- The ways teachers work together to improve classes and enjoy each other's company
- The importance of recruiting and selecting only the best teachers available
- The importance of varied, quality cocurricular activities to provide choices that meet the needs of all students
- The ability of teachers to make a difference in the lives of students

It is useful for leaders to know cultural stories and to become storytellers themselves.

ACTIVITIES ON HOW TO USE STORYTELLING

Develop Better School Stories

All of us can become better storytellers. Here are some suggestions for improving your school's stories. Learn how to tell a good story, and identify an important narrative you want to get across or improve on a piece of lore you already recount.

Several features of good stories can help improve the lore of any school. Here are some pointers (adapted from Deal and Key, 1998; Kouzes and Posner, 1999):

1. Pick a story that communicates deep values or purpose.
2. Paint word pictures with rich, descriptive language.
3. Be sincere, and tell it from the heart. Mean what you say.
4. Describe the people, the actions, and the situation.
5. Communicate your values through the story without preaching or lecturing.
6. Be simple, brief, and clear.
7. Describe how things worked out and what it means to the school and to you.
8. Practice the story, and know what are the most important elements.
9. Know your audience and how they will interpret the story's message.

In the space that follows, write an important story of your school.

Our Story

_____

_____

_____

_____

_____

_____

_____

_____

_____

_____

Assess the Purposes of Stories

Stories do many things for organizational culture. They teach what to do, mobilize people to act, and motivate the hearts and minds of staff and students (Kouzes and Posner, 1999). Negative stories can have a devastating effect. They can teach the wrong things to do, cause organizational anxiety, depress action, and decrease motivation and will. Once you have identified key stories, try to determine the impact of stories on staff, students, and community.

Story 1:

_____

_____

_____

_____

_____

Core message:

_____

_____

_____

Impact on staff, students, and community:

_____

_____

_____

Story 2:

_____

_____

_____

_____

_____

Core message:

_____

_____

_____

Impact on staff, students, and community:

_____

_____

_____

Story 3:

_____

_____

_____

_____

_____

_____

Core message:

_____

_____

_____

Impact on staff, students, and community:

_____

_____

_____

Story 4:

_____

_____

_____

_____

_____

Core message:

_____

_____

_____

Impact on staff, students, and community:

_____

_____

_____

Expand Storytelling Opportunities in Your School

Here are some ways to increase storytelling in a school. Pick one you might want to use.

- Hold a storytelling contest.
- At the beginning of the year, talk about the school history through stories.
- Audiotape and videotape key stories about the school, and make these available in the school library.
- Identify specific times to tell stories, such as at faculty meetings, during morning announcements, in the newsletter, during faculty retreats, before special planning meetings, and at the end of the year.
- Keep track of the key stories in a book, on a CD-ROM, in a videotape library, or on audiotape.
- Make the stories available to new members of the school and community when they arrive.
- Develop a "best of the best": keep the top ten stories available.

SHARED LANGUAGE

The use of words and language permeates the entire social context. Language is a cornerstone of any culture.

In schools, a special professional language and other unique words and phrases bind people together, keep outsiders at bay, and reinforce core values. All strong cultures share a unique language of special terms, acronyms, lingo, slang, argot, inside jokes, and unique names for places, people, or events. Leaders need to understand the language of their school's "tribe" and use that language to reinforce or transform cultural ways.

A prime requisite to symbolic leadership is to know and understand the school's lingo. Some language may be clear, decipherable, and obvious; other aspects may have hidden meanings and messages.

ACTIVITIES FOR UNCOVERING THE REAL MEANINGS OF WORDS AND PHRASES

Identify Slogans, Mottoes, and Special Phrases

Many slogans and mottoes are used in schools—for example,

All Children Can Learn

We Share, We Dare, We Care

Every Child a Promise

The Correlates

What is the shorthand used to talk about mission, future, and programs?

_____

_____

_____

Make a list of acronyms used in your school (for example, POPS, DARE, SAT, DEAR, ASCD, NAESP, NASSP, NSDC). Why are these acronyms used? Do they have positive or negative connotations?

_____

_____

_____

_____

_____

_____

Describe Events with Special Names

Schools often have special labels for traditions or ceremonies for students, staff, and parents. An example is referring to "holding an advance" rather than "holding a retreat." At Ganado Primary School in Ganado, Arizona, staff and students hold many events to build professional community. They have "Once Upon a Time Breakfasts" and "Curriculum Conversations."

List specially named events at your school. How did the name of the event originate? What is its deeper meaning?

_____

_____

_____

_____

_____

_____

List Nicknames for People, Places, or Programs

Language can label parts of the culture that are dysfunctional as well. Some words or phrases are meant in jest; others are just mean. But whether in jest or scorn, they always communicate interpretations about people or events. Here are some examples:

Lounge Lizards

Dr. Memo [a new principal who liked to send lots of memos]

Dr. Ditto [a staff member from the movie Teachers _who taught only through dittoed handouts]_

The Curriculum Queens

The Young Turks

The Old Fogies

The Mavericks

What are nicknames for people, places, or programs? Are these positive or negative? What makes these names special? What do they signify?

_____

_____

_____

_____

_____

Identify Negative Mottoes or Other Pejorative Language

Some schools develop negative or pejorative words for people, programs, or events that can reinforce negativity and a culture's toxic aspects. For example, in one school, the governance team was composed of four staff members who tried to take over all decision making. They became known as the Gang of Four.

If your school has negative words, how did these come into existence? Why are they still in use? How is the school's culture helped or harmed by these negative messages?

_____

_____

_____

_____

_____

Idea: Collect a list of common, positive language, lingo, names, and mottoes used in your school. Have them artfully written in calligraphy and framed for the front hall or the school homepage.

Idea: Develop an informal dictionary of words, acronyms, and lingo used in the school. One district had over twenty-five different acronyms alone, not counting program titles, unit descriptions, and building names.

Idea: Have students collect the "creation stories" of a phrase that tells how it came into being.

Idea: Positive, meaningful words and their definitions could become a small dictionary or booklet that is handed out to new staff members so they understand what is being said and can feel they are insiders.

Idea: Prepositions and pronouns also convey implicit meanings. "They work for me" is different from "They work with me." "My school is a special place" specifies something quite different from "Our school is a special place." Paying attention to the subtexts of language provides revealing clues to help discern cultural patterns and ways.

Write a dictionary of your school's special language:

A Dictionary of Language

_____

_____

_____

_____

_____

_____

_____

_____

_____

_____

_____

Architecture, Artifacts, and Symbols

The Visual Scene

ARCHITECTURE AND ENVIRONMENT

Where we work and learn has a powerful impact. Architecture and the physical environment affect our emotional state and our ability to concentrate, and they communicate beliefs about what is important.

In subtle yet significant ways, architecture and the physical environment play key cultural roles. They can

- Send messages about what is important. For example, is the football stadium state-of-the-art while the library is crumbling?

- Reinforce a sense of community. For example, does exhibited artwork reflect the ethnic and social diversity of the community?

- Communicate core mission and values. For example, are the spaces for learning as large as the spaces for play?

- Motivate hard work and pride. For example, does the school recognize and display the successful accomplishments of students, staff, and community members?

The physical setting, as part of the culture, influences our psychic state. If we work in a place that is dark and dirty, we are likely to feel emotionally drained, unhappy, and generally depressed. In contrast, in settings that are clean, decorated with attention to color and light, and with students' work displayed prominently, we are likely to feel upbeat, positive, and proud to be part of the school. Certainly, tight budgets can make it hard to keep buildings and grounds looking their best, but it is important to remember that beauty and style do not always carry a high price tag.

ACTIVITIES FOR LOOKING AT THE ARCHITECTURE AND THE PHYSICAL ENVIRONMENT

Every building communicates something through its use of light, space, and layout. And how people adorn the walls with signs, posters, and student work adds patina that affects how people react to the school.

Here are some questions to ask as you walk through a building:

- Is student work displayed in a prominent place?

- Is the school building beautified through the use of art, color, light, and plants?

- Is the hard work of students, staff, and others usefully recognized and celebrated?

- Is the core mission reinforced through banners, mottoes, exhibits, and presentations of accomplishments?

- Is the building clean, orderly, and pleasant?

- Do architectural elements communicate purpose and value?

- What is the school like when students are in class, passing in the hallways, hanging out after school?

- How do different spaces feel to you—energetic, sociable, threatening?

SYMBOLS

> Symbols represent intangible cultural values and beliefs. They are the outward manifestation of those things we cannot comprehend on a conscious level. They are expressions of shared sentiments and sacred commitment. Symbols infuse an organization with meaning.
>
> —Deal and Peterson, 1999, p. 60

Symbols are representations of deeper values and beliefs. They depict or signal core values and build affiliation with others in the school. As expressions of shared sentiments and sacred commitment, they tie people together and reinforce purpose.

Symbols are cultural icons that often represent potent intangibles. The architecture of the school can convey values. The display of artifacts can signal the history of students and staff. Leaders can symbolize vision and values through their words and deeds. They signal what is important by acting and speaking symbolically.

The Power of Symbols

Symbols are key to establishing cultural cohesion and pride. Positive use of symbols can unify a group; negative symbols can fragment an existing culture. Understanding and using existing symbols of a school can help maintain core values. Ignorance of cultural symbols can quickly destroy the trust in and credibility of leaders and damage existing values. It is key to learn about and understand the core symbols of the school and the artifacts of its past.

In designing buildings, creating displays, writing mottoes, or choosing logos, leaders should be mindful of the signals and messages being communicated. Symbols often play a more important role in schools than leaders initially suspect.

Living Logos

Principals and other leaders send powerful symbolic messages as they engage in seemingly mundane daily routines. They are what we call *living logos,* transmitting meaning and values in their words, actions, and nonverbal signals. The daily actions of every formal and informal leader become a placard, poster, or banner of core values and beliefs.

This symbolic signaling is evident in what they wear, the words they choose, problems they raise, innovations they suggest, things they feel deeply about, and what they pay attention to or ignore (Schein, 1985; Deal and Peterson, 1999). Other signals come from educational books they buy, read, and talk about; workshops and conferences they attend; things they notice when visiting a classroom; and things they write about. All leaders are living logos.

Examples of Symbols from Schools

There are many types of symbols in schools. Following are some examples:

- In an urban school, student papers are simply but elegantly matted with colored construction paper to heighten attractiveness.

- In a western high school, student work of all types—student poetry readings, athletic contests, plays, and written work—has been videotaped and is continually on view on a television set in the main office.

- In a Florida middle school, the new glass display cases house both athletic and academic awards, with the academic awards at eye level and the athletic trophies below.

- Audubon Elementary in Baton Rouge, Louisiana, has a Hall of Honor where the school has matted and framed newspaper articles mentioning teachers, poems published by students and staff, awards received for excellent teaching, and other accomplishments.

The following examples of symbols thus cover a range of possibilities:

- Logos
- Mascots
- Displays of student work
- Banners
- Displays of past achievements—athletic, academic, artistic, service
- Symbols of diversity
- Awards, trophies, and plaques
- Halls of honor (athletic, academic, artistic, service)
- Mission statements
- Historical artifacts and collections

ACTIVITIES FOR ASSESSING SYMBOLISM
Consider the School's Symbols and Artifacts
What are the school's symbols and artifacts? Where are they displayed and used? What do they mean?

_____

_____

_____

_____

_____

_____

_____

_____

Does the display of the symbols or artifacts reflect a positive message? If not, how might you change the display?

_____

_____

_____

_____

_____

Assess the Symbolism of Actions and Events

Symbolism is found in artifacts, actions, and events. Following is a list of different types of symbolic actions and events, along with a set of reflective questions to ask yourself.

The symbolism of action. What do you spend time doing? What do you avoid?

_____

_____

_____

_____

_____

The symbolism of the school tour. Where do you visit on the tour? What do you focus on when you visit a classroom? What does this communicate?

_____

_____

_____

_____

The symbolism of intellectual engagement. What ideas, readings, and issues do you engage yourself in learning?

_____

_____

_____

_____

The symbolism of writing. What do memos and messages from the principal's office communicate? Are they well formatted, clear, and engaging?

_____

_____

_____

_____

The symbolism of communicating ideas. What educational ideas do you champion?

_____

_____

_____

_____

The symbolism of advocacy. What do you take a stand on? What is important to fight for?

_____

_____

_____

_____

The symbolism of sharing and collegial relationships. What are the times and places for colleagues to gather together to share ideas, a meal, a concern, or a problem? Are these positive times of interaction and supportive relationships?

_____

_____

_____

_____

The symbolism of greetings. How are new and existing members greeted? Are the greetings warm and engaging?

_____

_____

_____

_____

The symbolism of song and music. How are songs and music used in the school? What do the lyrics communicate? Does the music reflect the diversity of the school?

_____

_____

_____

_____

The symbolism of joy, laughter, fun, humor. How are fun and laughter part of the school day?

_____

_____

_____

_____

The symbolism of storytelling. What stories are told? When are they told?

_____

_____

_____

_____

_____

The symbolism of recognition. How are people recognized for their accomplishments, hard work, and dedication?

_____

_____

_____

_____

The symbolism of professional learning. What is the nature of professional development? Is it a central part of the culture? When and how often does it occur?

_____

_____

_____

_____

ARTIFACTS IN THE SCHOOL: SYMBOLS AND SIGNS WITH MEANING

Every school has a wide spectrum of artifacts located in classrooms, hallways, and meeting places. Artifacts exist as symbols and signs of school values. Classrooms store symbols of work and learning. Hallways display a mix of student and teacher accomplishments, awards, messages, and mottoes. Meeting places often herald spirit and community in murals and mascots. For example, in Joyce Elementary School in Detroit, the enlarged mission statement is displayed in the front hall where everyone walking in can see it. In some schools, the core values of the school are on pins that staff members and students receive for special accomplishments.

Artifacts that recognize the accomplishments of staff, students, and community members motivate effort, focus attention on core values, and shout out that the school has done good, if not great, things.

Leaders need to help find, display, and organize the artifacts of the school into symbols and signs of purpose and value.

ASSESSING THE MEANING OF ARTIFACTS, SYMBOLS, AND SIGNS

Take some time to reflect on the artifacts, symbols, and signs in your school. Assess their meaning to staff, students, and community.

Examine the Mission Statement

Following are some questions to ask concerning your school's mission statement:

- Is the school mission statement prominently and engagingly displayed?

- Is it regularly refined and continually mentioned by leaders and staff members?

- Is the mission statement exhibited in the central meeting place of the school either in whole or as a motto or slogan?

Consider Displays of Student Work and Accomplishments

The visual display of student work and other student accomplishments is a central part of a school's culture. These displays, like those of a nation's museums, recognize what people can achieve. Consider your own school:

- Are there display cases of students' work, trophies, and artifacts of special efforts (footballs, notes from forensics, pom-poms, lab books from the Westinghouse Science winner)?

- Does the student work on classroom walls show what routine accomplishments look like? Are these regularly updated with newer accomplishments?

Display Banners, Murals, Wall Hangings, and Posters

Some schools prefer a sterile look; others articulate vision and values through larger wall displays. Banners crafted of cloth with words and symbols are powerful ways to reinforce values. Murals can bring together the work of students and others to send key messages about diversity, community service, and commitment. Wall hangings provide an opportunity to brighten up a dull hallway. Posters call attention to plays and movies but are also a way to signify values and success.

At Ganado Primary School in Arizona, Navajo rugs woven in the unique local red design are prominently displayed throughout the school. One particularly large and beautiful rug in the front hall served as the pattern for architects who designed the floor in the lunchroom.

At Muir Elementary School in Madison, Wisconsin, a large, complex bas-relief mural in the main office depicts major aspects of John Muir's world. The values of the school are embedded and reflected in the mural.

Ask yourself what banners and posters in your school are communicating. What is the school signaling and celebrating through larger visual displays?

Use Displays of Achievements, Triumphs, and Success

Most people want to be part of a winning organization. We feel greater motivation and commitment when we know we are part of a successful school. One of the key ways is to display past accomplishments around the school.

Ask yourself these questions about your school:

- Are there displays of both academic and athletic accomplishments?

- Do they communicate the importance of the accomplishments?

- Are the accomplishments attainable by most people, or are they only accomplishments of incredible achievement (Olympic Medals, Westinghouse Science Winners) that few could attain? Superachievers should be noted, but others must be recognized as well.

Collect and Examine Artifacts

Collecting and examining school artifacts is both important and fun, but it is often difficult to discern the meaning of artifacts in one's own culture. Following are some ways to collect them and interpret their meaning.

Imagine that you are an archeologist who has stumbled on a long-lost ruin that has been hidden in the sands for hundreds or even thousands of years. Walk around the school as though you have just opened up a long-closed building looking for artifacts and relics that seem important to the prior inhabitants. Be aware that some artifacts may be communicating significant messages.

What strikes your eye as you walk into classrooms?

_____

_____

_____

_____

_____

What do you find in hallways? What is the significance of these items?

_____

_____

_____

_____

_____

What key artifacts, artwork, posters, or other relics do you find in the main office? What messages do they communicate?

_____

_____

_____

_____

_____

Look for large rooms. What do you find in them? How were they used? For example, were they libraries, athletic training rooms, or theater settings?

_____

_____

_____

_____

Whose pictures are displayed? What do you think they represent about the school?

_____

_____

_____

_____

Identify the Most Important Artifacts

Engage the staff in a simulation to see what artifacts they consider important. Ask them to imagine that a fire is sweeping through the school. Luckily, all their teaching materials and records have already been saved, but they need to decide what else is important enough to save.

What should be salvaged for posterity first?

_____

_____

_____

What else would they want to be sure to rescue if they could?

_____

_____

_____

Why are these things important to the school?

_____

_____

_____

What would be important artifacts to help them rebuild a history of the school?

_____

_____

_____

_____

What things should be left behind because it would be better to start anew without them?

_____

_____

_____

_____

On a day when the school is empty, walk into the building from the doors that students use. Look at what you see first. What message do you get from the setting? Try to sense what the building is like as you enter it. Is it warm? Threatening? Cold and dark? Cheery and fun?

_____

_____

_____

_____

Conduct an Educational Garage Sale

Determining what aspects of the culture to keep and celebrate and what aspects to transform or change is key to maintaining a strong, professional culture. One way to approach this is to conduct an "educational garage sale" in which staff members select aspects of the school to store, sell, or trade.

For the sale, staff members will determine what to do with various aspects of the school. Things for the garage sale can include values, programs, equipment, past events, social relationships, curricular ideas, teaching approaches, educational issues, and conflicts. Although these are not directly cultural elements, nonetheless each represents sets of norms or values in the school.

Here are some possibilities for the items that can be collected:

- Some items will be placed in a *museum* because they have served the school well and need a place of honor, but should no longer be part of the school. An example is the old spelling series.

- Some items are *not for sale* because they are positive features of the school. An example is a successful reading or writing program.

- Some items are not highly valued and might be *sold or bartered* to some other school or group. An example is the school's computer equipment, which is still somewhat functional but people would gladly trade.

- Some items cannot be sold or bartered and should simply be thrown in the *garbage can*. These are things that do not work well or are of no use in the current school. An example is the old assemblies that no longer motivate students or the textbooks that are out-of-date.

- Some items are highly negative and toxic. These must be handled carefully and deposited into a *toxic waste hauler*. Examples are the longtime conflicts among staff members, the negative expectations held about some students, or the hostility that arises in faculty meetings.

Staff members are to reflect on aspects of the school they want to keep, sell, or get rid of. Either write the names of the categories on separate chart papers or draw a simple picture to represent the category (a museum, a garbage can, and the others). Tape the chart papers with the categories on the wall.

Next, have each staff member write the name of items they want to save, sell, or get rid of on paper. Have staff members tape their items to the chart that represents what they want done with it. If you have multicolored paper for the items, you will end up with a wall of chart paper and rainbow-colored items.

Once everyone has put up all their items, have everyone tour the various categories to see how others feel. Later, type up the lists and find ways to address the items that should be changed (those in the garbage can or toxic waste hauler) and find ways to celebrate the items that are not for sale.

List your items for each category.

Museum

_____

_____

_____

_____

_____

_____

_____

Not for Sale

_____

_____

_____

_____

_____

_____

_____

Sale or Barter

_____
_____
_____
_____
_____
_____
_____

Garbage Can

_____
_____
_____
_____
_____
_____
_____

Toxic Waste Hauler

_____
_____
_____
_____
_____
_____
_____

Shaping
School Culture

Assessing and Transforming Toxic Cultures

T oxic cultures or negative subcultures can be quite destructive to a school—to its staff morale or student learning, for example. To understand the nature of toxic cultures, it is important to understand how they differ from positive places.

In positive cultures, one finds an underlying set of norms and values, history and stories, hopes and dreams that are productive, encouraging, and optimistic. Positive relationships abound around a strong sense of connection to the core mission.

Positive cultures have these characteristics (Deal and Peterson, 1999):

- A mission focused on student and teacher learning

- A rich sense of history and purpose

- Core values of collegiality, performance, and improvement that engender quality, achievement, and learning

- Positive beliefs and assumptions about the potential of students and staff to learn and grow

- A strong professional community that uses knowledge, experience, and research to improve practice

- A shared sense of responsibility for student outcomes

- A cultural network that fosters positive communication flows
- Leadership among staff and administrators that blends continuity with improvement
- Rituals and ceremonies that reinforce core cultural values
- Stories that celebrate successes and recognize heroines and heroes
- An overall sense of interpersonal connection, meaningful purpose, and belief in the future
- A physical environment that symbolizes joy and pride
- A widely shared sense of respect and caring for everyone

It is not possible to talk about school culture without attending to its negative possibilities. Most schools enjoy somewhat positive cultures, but some are gripped by a set of negative norms and values. Negative cultural patterns are built over time as a staff works together, fights together, and, in many cases, fails together. In positive cultures, these natural challenges are faced openly and dealt with; in negative cultures, these challenges fester and grow into dysfunctional attributes.

Toxic cultures or subcultures dampen enthusiasm, reduce professionalism, and depress organizational effectiveness. Leaders must address these negative elements in order for the school to thrive.

Toxic cultures have these characteristics (Deal and Peterson, 1999):

- A lack of shared purpose or a splintered mission based on self-interest
- Staff members who find most of their meaning in activities outside work, negativity, or antistudent sentiments
- Viewing the past as a story of defeat and failure
- Norms of radical individualism, the acceptance of mediocrity, and an avoidance of innovation
- Little sense of community where negative beliefs about colleagues and students abound
- Few positive traditions or ceremonies to develop a sense of community

- A cultural network of naysayers, saboteurs, rumormongers, and antiheroes, where communication is primarily negative
- A dearth of leadership in the principal's office and among staff
- Positive role models unrecognized in the school and community
- Social connections that have become fragmented and openly antagonist
- Rather than hopes, dreams, and a clear vision, a sense of hopelessness, discouragement, and despair

These settings are unpleasant places to work in because staff members often have become accustomed to the negativity and have adapted to the toxic environment. In addition, the negativity is reinforced by the cultural network of naysayers and saboteurs. It is sometimes difficult for them to see their own pathology, let alone change it.

What leaders can do is always shaped by the context. Leaders need to ask themselves: How toxic is the workplace? Are there potential leaders who can pull the school together? Was there ever a time when the community pulled together in a positive way? Usually, there is at least a small core of optimistic people who want to turn the culture around.

Working with toxic cultures and subcultures is absolutely crucial to establishing a stronger, more productive school. A number of principals and teachers have pointed out to us that it takes only a few powerful, negative people to drag the school down.

THE ORIGIN OF TOXIC CULTURES AND SUBCULTURES

Toxic cultures form the same way that positive cultures form. Over time, as the staff and leaders face challenges, try to solve problems, and cope with tragedy and difficulty, they build up negative views of their work, their abilities, and their students. In part, negative cultures develop because there is no leadership to help staff members overcome adversity, avoid negative rationalizations, and provide positive closure to conflict.

The drift toward negativity is often a slow, gradual process that even positive people are not aware of. But over time, negative views of work take over and become the shared way of viewing the school. And also over time, the culture starts to reinforce its own negatively. As we have noted,

> In toxic schools, the elements of culture reinforce negativity. Values and beliefs are negative. The cultural network works in opposition to anything positive. Rituals and traditions are phony, joyless, or counterproductive.
> —Deal and Peterson, 1999, p. 119

ACTIVITIES FOR READING, ASSESSING, AND TRANSFORMING NEGATIVE ASPECTS OF THE CULTURE

The suggested activities that follow for reading negative cultural patterns and ways to assess and transform the negative features can become an assessment activity by simply asking this important question: "What aspects of the culture do we find positive and supportive of our shared mission, and what aspects do we feel are negative and hinder the accomplishment of our mission?"

Identify Toxic Subcultures

Most schools are not universally toxic; rather, they have pockets of negativity. There may be a grade level, department, or group of people who are keepers of the negative. These are not the honest and helpful critics who help the school avoid mistakes. They are the constantly and continually cynical who use complaints to gain power and attention.

Look for any groups or subgroups who take a consistently negative perspective on the school or its activities yet seem unwilling to work to improve what they view as not working. Look also for keepers of the nightmare, who remind the staff of everything that hasn't turned out well, rumormongers who share only gloom, hostile storytellers who pass on dismal history, and antiheroines or antiheroes who are harmful exemplars. Who is in the negative subculture or subcultures? What are the negative aspects they focus on?

As a leader, you might want to point out to the negative subcultures their pessimistic views and try to understand how they developed their views. Ask if they would serve on a committee to work to ameliorate the situation. If it is a situation that cannot change—for example, state standards, the type of students in the school, the socioeconomic level of the parents—point out that there is no way to change these, and work with them on addressing things they have control over.

Leaders could conduct a search for negative groups in order to understand who they are, what they stand for, and why they are so regularly disapproving. Leaders need to know and understand the negativity. Ask yourself the following questions in order to learn about these groups.

Who are the members of the negative group?

_____

_____

_____

_____

_____

_____

_____

What is the focus of the negativity?

_____

_____

_____

_____

_____

_____

_____

_____

What is the possible historical source of the negativity?

_____

_____

_____

_____

_____

_____

What are some ways to work with the group to address their concerns?

_____

_____

_____

_____

_____

_____

Listen to and Transform Toxic Stories

Most schools have stories of plans that did not work out, ideas that floundered, and programs that failed (they died or lost their funding). Positive cultures use these stories to learn from. Negative cultures use failure stories to reinforce a negative view of the school. Be assured that there will be some truth in the story. The meaning attached to the story and its consequences are the significant aspects.

Negative stories should be learned and addressed directly. Describe the negative stories of the school. Identify the message of the story (both its truth and its meaning), and then list two or three ways you plan to address the story.

Story 1:

_____

_____

_____

_____

_____

_____

Message in the story:

_____

_____

_____

_____

Plan to address the main message:

_____

_____

_____

_____

_____

Story 2:

_____

_____

_____

_____

_____

_____

_____

Message in the story:

_____

_____

_____

_____

Plan to address the main message:

_____

_____

_____

_____

_____

Story 3:

_____

_____

_____

_____

_____

_____

_____

Message of the story:

_____

_____

_____

_____

_____

Plan to address the main message:

_____

_____

_____

_____

_____

_____

Deal with Specific Toxic Elements

Staff, administrators, and sometimes students in the upper grades all have a responsibility to address toxic cultures. Following are some problems and approaches to solving them. These are followed by activities and reflective questions to consider.

Toxic Element: A Lack of Shared Purpose

Suggested action: Identify the core mission and purpose of the school, and find ways to reinforce that sense of purpose.

Activities: Use many of the activities already described in this book. Return to the prior chapters and examine the next chapter for specific activities that look at what the core mission is and ways to reinforce it. The more the mission is communicated, celebrated, and discussed, the more it will become shared. Describe aspects of the mission that are shared and those that are not shared.

_____

_____

_____

_____

_____

_____

Toxic Element: Staff Members Who Find Most of Their Meaning in Outside Activities or Negativity

Suggested action: Have staff members develop action plans for their personal mission and the school mission.

Activity: Have each staff member develop a personal mission statement, then list specific actions he or she will take to accomplish the personal mission as well as actions to accomplish the shared mission of the school. In small groups of four or five staff members each, have everyone share their missions and their plans. These plans could be developed at the end of the summer or early in the semester, put into a self-addressed envelope, and sent in January as a reminder of what each staff member had planned to accomplish. Describe how you will foster a shared sense of mission.

_____

_____

_____

_____

_____

_____

Toxic Element: Viewing the Past as a Story of Defeat and Failure

Suggested action: Openly address the problems of the past, but then focus on current successes, no matter how small, and make clear plans to avoid the errors of the past.

Activities: Break the staff into small groups of four or five. Have them list all the accomplishments of the past on one sheet of chart paper and all the mistakes or failures on another. Discuss the accomplishments. List specific actions to take in order to avoid the same mistakes in the future. Develop an action plan for doing this and write it down here.

_____

_____

_____

_____

_____

Note: In schools with a history of failed leadership, poor planning, and disorganization, this activity can be difficult because so many problems are brought up. In this situation, leaders should informally learn about past mistakes and begin to address them in their plans and decisions. Once there is a more positive climate, this type of anthropological dig can be less destructive. Overall, when schools have had many failures, a great deal of healing is needed.

Toxic Element: Little Sense of Community

Suggested action: Build a sense of community by celebrating contributions, developing relationships, articulating the shared purposes and values of the school, and establishing respectful, trusting, caring relationships.

Activities

- Increase opportunities (during faculty meetings, at pep rallies, in daily communications) for staff members to celebrate their own and others' contributions.

- Increase the number and quality of informal interactions among staff members, such as potluck meals, playing games together, time to share personal and professional ideas, and scheduled outings together.

- Develop a list of belief statements about staff, student, and community relationships with a focus on how to reinforce respectful, trusting, caring relationships. List the belief statements on chart paper and identify the behaviors that demonstrate those type of relationships.

- Organize a "Sunshine Club" that truly provides sunshine to staff members in need. Describe what the group would do to effectively support staff needs.

_____

_____

_____

_____

**Toxic Element: Few Positive Traditions or
Ceremonies That Develop a Sense of Community**

Suggested action: Review the traditions and ceremonies that occur over the year, and determine whether they are all positive, celebratory experiences. Design and implement new ceremonies that celebrate the positive, active parts of the culture.

Activity: After completing the yearly analysis of traditions and ceremonies, look for gaps in the year or the existence of negative or dead traditions. Develop new, enriching traditions to build and reinforce a sense of community.

Reflective questions

- Do you have numerous traditions and ceremonies that communicate and reinforce the core of positive norms, values, and accomplishments?

- Do you need to end some negative traditions or enhance some ineffective traditions or ceremonies?

- What specific ceremonies can you make into powerful, community-building, energizing, and motivating experiences? Describe how you would do this.

_____

_____

_____

_____

_____

_____

_____

_____

_____

Toxic Element: A Cultural Network That Is Constantly Negative and Hostile

Suggested action: Provide direct, nonjudgmental feedback about specific negative behaviors and their effect on the school and its staff. Buffer newly hired staff members from negative members of the culture, or they will be socialized into the toxic subculture. Provide new staff members with positive, supportive mentors.

Activity: Identify a member of the staff who takes on negative roles, and provide informal feedback and, if necessary, formal feedback about how his or her behavior is affecting the group. Do some coaching on how to change the person's behavior, offer to send him or her to a workshop on collaboration or effective teamwork, or bring in a consultant to work with the person on transforming negative actions into positive ones.

Reflective questions

- Who on the staff regularly criticizes everything that is done? (These are not the honest and helpful critics who point out problems in plans, budgets, or ideas that should be considered.)

- What impact does this behavior have on others?

- What can you say to give them specific, nonjudgmental feedback about the effect of their behavior?

_____

_____

_____

_____

_____

_____

_____

_____

_____

Idea: "Plant new trees" by hiring new staff members who support positive values and know how to work collaboratively.

Toxic Element: A Lack of Leadership in the School

Suggested action: Work to improve your own leadership and nurture leadership among the staff.

Activities

- Conduct a self-evaluation, asking whether you are engaging in the roles and actions described in this and other books on leadership. Note areas of accomplishment and areas for improvement.

- Next, do an informal assessment of staff leadership. Who are seen as leaders? When do they have opportunities to lead? How are they recognized for their leadership?

- Then ask staff members whom they see as leaders; discuss the importance of staff leadership during a retreat or faculty meeting. Ask the staff what everyone can do to encourage staff leadership in the school. Take the suggestions, and use the best ones.

- Finally, develop an action plan for building and supporting staff leadership through empowerment, new decision-making structures, professional development, and recognition of staff leaders. Describe what you would do month by month.

_____

_____

_____

_____

_____

_____

_____

_____

_____

_____

_____

_____

_____

_____

_____

_____

_____

_____

Toxic Element: Positive Role Models Remain Unrecognized in the School and Community

Suggested action: There are always some staff members who are dedicated teachers; find them. Support and recognize these staff members.

Activities

- Identify staff members who have conducted themselves in positive and professional ways. Initially, recognize them confidentially for their contributions. If they will not be criticized by negative staff members, tell their stories to the school during faculty meetings, in the school newsletter, or on the principal's daily tours.

- List ways in which you can recognize the school's role models.

_____

_____

_____

_____

_____

_____

_____

Toxic Element: The Only Exemplars Are Antiheroic and Negative Role Models

Suggested action: Recognize and acknowledge the contributions of positive, energizing staff members.

Reflective questions

- Who are your negative role models? Why is their negative behavior respected or valued? How did they become negative role models? Describe how you might address the negative behavior.

  _____

  _____

  _____

  _____

- Who can you identify as positive role models and exemplars of the school's values? Describe how you can acknowledge their contributions.

  _____

  _____

  _____

  _____

  _____

  _____

Toxic Element: Rather Than Hopes, Dreams, and a Clear Vision, the Culture Supports a Sense of Hopelessness, Discouragement, and Despair

Suggested action: Articulate a clear, compelling, and positive vision for the school. Make the vision a reality by developing plans, taking action, and modeling its importance. Reinforce that vision by communicating it in stories, words, and "walking the talk."

Activities: Hold positive, well-designed ceremonies to recognize positive accomplishments related to the school's vision.

Reflective questions

- Is there a clear, compelling, and positive vision for the school that is regularly articulated?

- Are there plans and actions that are moving the school forward?

- How can staff and administration reinforce and communicate the vision to everyone?

_____

_____

_____

_____

_____

_____

_____

_____

_____

_____

_____

_____

_____

Understanding and dealing with negative, toxic cultures is a challenge. Following is an overview of major strategies that leaders have used to deal with toxic cultures or subcultures (Deal and Peterson, 1999).

Strategies for Overcoming Negativism

- Confront the negativity head-on; give people a chance to vent their venom in a public forum.
- Shield and support positive cultural elements and staff members.
- Focus energy on the recruitment, selection, and retention of effective, positive staff members.
- Help those who might succeed and thrive better in a new district make the move to a new school.
- Consciously and directly focus on eradicating the negative and rebuilding around positive norms and beliefs.
- Develop new stories of success, renewal, and accomplishment.
- End old or dead ceremonies, and revive dying, decrepit ones.
- Celebrate the positive and the possible.

Eight Roles of Symbolic Leaders

School principals take on many different roles. They are managers, working to keep the school running smoothly by attending to the school's structures and activities, policies and procedures, resources and programs, and rules and standards. They also play a central role in shaping culture by articulating values, communicating the vision, recognizing accomplishments, and sustaining traditions. The most successful principals are "bifocal leaders," shaping culture in their managerial roles and smoothing functioning in their symbolic roles (Deal and Peterson, 1994).

As managers, principals take on eight major roles:

1. Organizational planners
2. Resource allocators
3. Coordinators of programs
4. Supervisors of staff and outcomes
5. Disseminators of ideas and information
6. Jurists who adjudicate disagreements and conflicts
7. Gatekeepers at the boundaries of the school
8. Analysts who use systematic approaches to address complex problems

As leaders, principals take on eight symbolic roles (Deal and Peterson, 1994):

1. Historians delving into stories of the past

2. Anthropological detectives uncovering current norms and values

3. Visionaries who articulate deeper purposes

4. Symbols communicating core values through actions and attention

5. Potters shaping culture by attending to rituals, traditions, and ceremonies

6. Poets using language to articulate core values and purpose

7. Actors taking on key roles in social dramas

8. Healers who minister to wounds that occur during loss, conflict, or tragedy

Both roles, managerial and symbolic, are key to building successful schools, and both sets of roles can shape the culture.

It is important for leaders to reflect on the various roles they play. In the following activities, you will be able to examine the culture-shaping roles you take on. In addition, you will be able see how you can shape the culture by combining your managerial and symbolic roles (Deal and Peterson, 1994, 1999):

- *Historian:* Seeks to understand the social and normative past of the school

- *Anthropological detective:* Probes for and analyzes the norms, values, and beliefs that define the current culture

- *Visionary:* Works with others to define a deeply value-based picture of the school's future

- *Symbol:* Affirms values through dress, behavior, attention, and routines

- *Potter:* Shapes and is shaped by heroes, rituals, traditions, ceremonies, and symbols; encourages the staff to share core values and dreams

- *Poet:* Uses language to reinforce values and sustain a positive image

- *Actor:* Improvises in a school's inevitable dramas, comedies, and tragedies

- *Healer:* Oversees transitions and change in the life of the school; heals the wounds of conflict and loss

REFLECTING ON THE ROLES YOU TAKE

Every leader takes on these eight roles in varying ways and at different times. Reflecting on when and how you take on these roles can strengthen your role as a culture shaper. Examine each role, and ask yourself which ones you take on by answering the reflective questions following each role.

Historian: Delves into stories of the past

How have you developed a detailed and deep account of the school's past?

_____

_____

_____

_____

_____

Do you have a keen sense of crises, challenges, and meaningful successes that have shaped the culture? What are these events?

_____

_____

_____

_____

_____

_____

_____

_____

Anthropological detective: Uncovers and analyzes current
norms and values

When do you encourage the storytellers on the staff and in the community to keep
you up on what's going on?

_____

_____

_____

_____

What are your regular routines that take the temperature of the current culture?

_____

_____

_____

_____

_____

Visionary: Articulates deeper purposes

What is your idea of what the school might become? How would you describe your
vision?

_____

_____

_____

_____

_____

_____

How have you worked to make an engaging, meaningful vision widely shared?

_____

_____

_____

_____

_____

_____

_____

In what ways do you use multiple verbal, written, and nonverbal ways to articulate and reinforce the vision?

_____

_____

_____

_____

_____

_____

_____

Having a vision for the school remains one of the most important things a leader can do. A vision should be clear, compelling, and connected to deep values about education and learning. You need to be able to articulate that vision in a variety of ways.

Examine your vision for the school:

What is a longer, more detailed description of the vision for the school that you and the staff share?

_____

_____

_____

_____

_____

What are the key components of the vision that can be communicated quickly and simply?

_____

_____

_____

_____

_____

Is there a motto or slogan that communicates part of the vision? What is it?

_____

_____

_____

_____

_____

How do you communicate the vision? It is important not only to have a clear and energizing collaboratively developed vision for the school. It must also be communicated in a variety of ways.

In what ways is the vision made visible? When and where?

_____

_____

_____

_____

_____

_____

_____

What are the major ceremonies where the vision is communicated? How is it communicated during the ceremony (by written, verbal, or symbolic means)?

_____

_____

_____

_____

_____

_____

_____

_____

How is the public informed of the vision? How do you communicate the vision to all the diverse elements of the community?

_____

_____

_____

_____

_____

_____

How is the informal network encouraged to communicate the vision? Who is part of the grapevine of communication?

_____

_____

_____

_____

Can staff members also articulate the vision? How do you know? How can you help them communicate more clearly or intensely?

_____

_____

_____

_____

_____

_____

What formal media are used to communicate the vision? How is the vision communicated by telephone, newsletters, memos, e-mail, faxes, school Web pages, the public address system, public access television, videotapes of the school, or outdoor displays?

_____

_____

_____

_____

_____

_____

_____

Symbol: Communicates core values through actions and attention

Do you have a set of routines and rituals that clearly communicate your values and vision? Which are most effective?

_____

_____

_____

_____

_____

_____

_____

How do you communicate verbally and through your actions your excitement about the school and its accomplishments?

_____

_____

_____

_____

What do your actions and emotions communicate symbolically? What do you pay attention to? What do you appreciate? What do you ignore or admonish (Schein, 1985)?

_____

_____

_____

_____

_____

_____

What messages do you communicate in your daily actions, classroom visits, and interactions?

_____

_____

_____

_____

_____

_____

How is your office decorated? What does your personal space communicate about your values and vision?

_____

_____

_____

_____

_____

_____

Idea: Take a photo of your office from the perspective of visitors. What do they see? What might they infer from what they see?

Potter: Shapes culture by attending to rituals, traditions, and ceremonies

Do you use recruitment and hiring as a way of communicating values and shaping the culture? What are your best techniques for selecting staff members who share the values of the school?

_____

_____

_____

_____

_____

_____

_____

Do you make decisions based on the values and mission of the school? Describe two examples.

_____

_____

_____

_____

_____

How do you celebrate and recognize the accomplishments of heroes and heroines? Do you encourage the staff's role models? Do you recognize the accomplishments of key staff members on a regular basis? When is this done?

_____

_____

_____

_____

_____

Do you observe ongoing rituals and maintain esprit de corps through ceremony and tradition? What are your best events to do this?

_____

_____

_____

_____

_____

Poet: Uses language to articulate core values and purposes

What language (spoken, written, displayed) do you use to reinforce core values? What key words are important to you?

_____

_____

_____

_____

_____

_____

_____

How do you use language to elevate the hopes and dreams of staff and students?

_____

_____

_____

_____

What are the stories you tell or encourage others to tell about the school?

_____

_____

_____

_____

_____

_____

Do you make storytelling a regular part of school life? When are the best times?

_____

_____

_____

_____

Do you nurture the poets on the staff who articulate the community's deepest felt values? Who are the best poets? Why are they so skilled?

_____

_____

_____

_____

_____

Actor: Takes on key roles in social dramas

What are the main "stages" on which you perform? How do you prepare to be on stage? What "costumes" are used for different roles?

_____

_____

_____

_____

_____

What roles do you assume during morning announcements, faculty meetings, and retirement ceremonies?

_____

_____

_____

_____

How do these roles communicate your values and vision?

_____

_____

_____

_____

_____

_____

Are there special ceremonies you encourage that communicate values through symbol, word, and ritual?

_____

_____

_____

_____

_____

_____

How might you amplify the deeper purposes of education in these ceremonies?

_____

_____

_____

_____

_____

_____

_____

_____

Healer: Ministers to wounds that occur during loss, conflict, or tragedy

How do you heal wounds that are the inevitable consequence of change? What are some of the ongoing wounds that faculty feel from past losses or difficulties?

_____

_____

_____

_____

_____

_____

_____

_____

How and when have you helped heal the wounds of past reforms, programs, or leaders that caused hurt?

_____

_____

_____

_____

_____

_____

_____

Do you encourage ceremonies that recognize key transitional events in the work lives of staff and students?

_____

_____

_____

_____

_____

_____

_____

How do you acknowledge the pain or difficulties of those who are trying to improve their work?

_____

_____

_____

_____

How have you helped cope with the sadness and grief as the community faced tragedy, loss, or the death of a member of the community?

_____

_____

_____

_____

_____

CULTURE-BUILDING ROLE ASSESSMENT

Think of the times you have assumed each role. For each role, describe when you took on the role and its impact on the school. If you overlooked some of the roles, ask yourself why and see if you should take on some alternative roles.

Historian

When do you take on the role?

_____

_____

What impact do you have?

_____

_____

_____

Anthropological Detective

When do you assume the role?

_____

_____

What impact do you have?

_____

_____

_____

Visionary

When do you try to articulate a vision for the school?

_____

_____

_____

What impact do you have?

_____

_____

_____

Symbol

When do your demeanor and actions stand out?

_____

_____

_____

What impact do you have?

_____

_____

_____

Potter

When do you try to shape cultural ways?

_____

_____

_____

What impact do you have?

_____

_____

_____

Poet

When do you try to articulate core values and beliefs?

_____

_____

What impact do you have?

_____

_____

_____

Actor

When do you take the stage?

_____

_____

_____

What impact do you have?

_____

_____

_____

Healer
When do you try to heal old wounds?

_____

_____

_____

What impact do you have?

_____

_____

_____

USING REGULAR EVENTS TO REINFORCE SCHOOL CULTURE

A number of yearly activities provide an excellent time to reinforce cultural values. Too often viewed as only administrative or technical events, each event can meaningfully reinforce core values. Ask yourself these questions:

- Do your *faculty meetings* build community, engender respect, and value professional problem solving?

- On the *school tour* around the building, do people connect, share, and praise each other?

- Are *budgeting and planning* times for recognizing and reinforcing the guiding principles of the school?

- Is *hiring* a careful process of selecting quality people, a first initiation into the culture, and a time to brag about the school?

- Are *parent conferences* a time of celebration, respectful feedback, and true shared communication?

- Are *school assemblies* well organized and planned so that they build ties among staff and students as well as school pride?

- At the *end of the year,* do the community and the staff come together to celebrate successes, grieve endings, and identify possibilities for the coming year?

CELEBRATING AND IMPROVING YOUR ROLES

No one is perfect in all eight roles. Those you are comfortable and successful in should be recognized and celebrated.

There are other roles each of us wants to improve, expand, or refine. We may not be comfortable in the role, or we might need more practice to be better at it.

Reflect on the ways you assume these eight roles. Give yourself credit for roles you take on effectively. But consider what you might do differently where you are less successful.

What roles are you best at? Which roles are you particularly effective at? Which ones do you want to improve or expand?

My best roles:

_____

_____

_____

_____

_____

_____

_____

_____

_____

Roles that might be improved or refined:

_____

_____

_____

_____

_____

_____

My next steps to enhance my roles:

_____

_____

_____

_____

_____

_____

_____

ACTION PLAN FOR DEVELOPING CULTURE-SHAPING ROLES

In the following pages, we have provided space for you to develop a set of action plans for your work. Although you are shaping the culture with your words and actions as you lead, thinking more systematically can help you become more reflective and more effective at shaping the culture. We encourage you to think about how you read, assess, and reinforce or transform the culture on a daily, weekly, or yearly basis. Develop some personal action plans.

Daily Action Plan

8:00 A.M.

Noon

3:30 P.M.

Weekly Action Plan

Monday

Tuesday

Wednesday

Thursday

Friday

Saturday

Sunday

Yearly Action Plan

August

September

October

November

December

January

February

March

April

May

June

July

FINAL THOUGHTS

School principals have a lot on their minds and even more on their plates. Each day is full of situations that demand immediate attention and land mines that can explode without warning. So where does a principal need to focus attention and take action? Many people believe that the technical aspects of schools—especially instruction—should be at the top of the priority list. This fieldbook offers another avenue. It is the culture of schools that really matters, and that is where principals need to devote much of their time and attention. Without a well-focused and cohesive set of cultural norms and values, a school is adrift, subject to the turbulent and ever-changing pressures dictating the next promising direction to take. Without a cultural compass, a school becomes a weather vane, with everyone dizzy and disoriented about where to head.

This fieldbook suggests three main things that principals need to do: (1) read cultural signs and clues; (2) assess what is working and what is not; and (3) where needed, change things for the better. The first duty casts principals in the role of anthropological detectives; the second emphasizes their analytic role; and the third moves them in the direction of potters, poets, or healers.

Reading Cultural Signposts

As we have pointed out, sizing up a culture does not require a degree in anthropology. It is a matter of stepping back and reading between the lines of daily events. All groups of people, over time, evolve a distinctive pattern of what is valued and how people should behave. Behind language, rituals, and folkways is a taken-for-granted set of assumptions that help people make sense of their lives at work. Every principal should take some time to decipher the symbolic glue that holds a school together. The easiest time to do this is when the principal is new and not yet indoctrinated into existing mores and norms. But it can also be done by any veteran who makes the commitment.

Assessing School Culture

Some lessons that cultures pass from generation to generation serve contemporary needs very well; other lessons have lost their meaning. When cultural patterns have little meaning, people go through the motions without emotion and find little to connect them to others or to the school. The school becomes a sterile environment where students, staff, and teachers just put in their time and find meaning elsewhere—in gangs, families, or part-time jobs.

Even worse, in some cultures, beliefs and practices are counterproductive. Although they may have served a purpose in the past, the old ways have become negative and destructive. They may still hold a group together, but the bonds are now toxic rather than productive. Once a principal gets a bead on the culture of a school, he or she can then try to figure out what is working and what is not. Successful practices need reinforcement and celebration; others need to be changed.

Changing School Culture

For the past several decades, nationwide efforts have focused on school reform. Most of these efforts have emphasized technical issues, with the intent of making schools more "rational"—cast more in the image of businesses (or what reformers think businesses are like). The reforms have been robust and costly; the results have been mixed. But the unintended consequences of wave upon wave of change have weakened the cultures of schools. Across the country, too many schools are sterile places where teachers make apologies for what they do: "I'm just a teacher." Other schools are toxic environments where people take glee in resisting improvements or sabotaging change. The real challenge for most principals is how to bring about change from the bottom up rather than simply following dictates imposed from the top. But that will take a deep view of what change entails.

In today's world, everyone is for change as long as they, or those around them, do not have to do anything differently. Change is like a trapeze act. You have to let go before you can grab on. If you let go too soon, you'll miss the next bar. If you hold on too long, you'll lose momentum.

We believe that the act of letting go is an essential step in moving on. This means that school principals will need to orchestrate collective wakes, funerals, mourning periods, and commemorative events to help heal cultural wounds caused by successions of change and reform. For most principals, the role of healer was not written into the formal job description. But we believe that it is one of the essential tasks of school leadership. You cannot shape new cultural values and traditions in a school landscape littered with past failures and shattered hopes and dreams. Too often, principals are told they need a vision when their schools are still wedded to an old history that needs to be jettisoned before people can latch on to a better future.

As you move ahead, be sure to reinforce the positive, meaningful elements of your school's culture while you find the energy to heal the wounds of toxic environments. Help return the cultural compass and sense of deep purpose to your school.

REFERENCES

Bower, M. *Will to Manage.* New York: McGraw-Hill, 1996.

Clark, B. "The Organizational Saga in Higher Education." *Administrative Science Quarterly,* 1972, *17,* 178–184.

Deal, T. E., and Kennedy, A. A. *Corporate Cultures: The Rites and Rituals of Corporate Life.* Reading, Mass.: Addison-Wesley, 1982.

Deal, T. E., and Key, M. K. *Corporate Celebration: Play, Purpose, and Profit at Work.* San Francisco: Berrett-Koehler, 1998.

Deal, T. E., and Peterson, K. D. *The Leadership Paradox: Balancing Logic and Artistry in Schools.* San Francisco: Jossey-Bass, 1994.

Deal, T. E., and Peterson, K. D. *Shaping School Culture: The Heart of Leadership.* San Francisco: Jossey-Bass, 1999.

Gordon, W. J. *Synectics: The Development of Creative Capacity.* New York: Collier Books, 1961.

Kouzes, J. M., and Posner, B. Z. *Encouraging the Heart: A Leader's Guide to Rewarding and Recognizing Others.* San Francisco: Jossey-Bass, 1999.

Kübler-Ross, E. *On Death and Dying.* New York: Macmillan, 1969.

Ott, J. S. *The Organizational Perspective.* Pacific Grove, Calif.: Brooks/Cole, 1989.

Schein, E. H. *Organizational Culture and Leadership.* San Francisco: Jossey-Bass, 1985.

Waller, W. *The Sociology of Teaching.* New York: Wiley, 1932.